Editor
Eric Migliaccio

Managing Editor
Ina Massler Levin, M.A.

Editor-in-Chief
Sharon Coan, M.S. Ed.

Illustrator
Bruce Hedges

Cover Artist
Brenda DiAntonis

Art Coordinator
Kevin Barnes

Imaging
Rosa C. See

Product Manager
Phil Garcia

Publishers
Rachelle Cracchiolo, M.S. Ed.
Mary Dupuy Smith, M.S. Ed.

Nonfiction Reading Comprehension

Grade

Geography

Science

History

Author

Debra J. Housel, M.S. Ed.

Teacher Created Materials, Inc.
6421 Industry Way
Westminster, CA 92683
www.teachercreated.com
ISBN-0-7439-3386-9
©2003 Teacher Created Materials, Inc.
Made in U.S.A.

Table of Contents

Introduction

Comprehension is the primary goal of any reading task. Students who comprehend expository text will have more opportunities in life as well as better test performance. Through the use of nonfiction passages followed by exercises that require vital reading and thinking skills, *Nonfiction Reading Comprehension* will help you to develop confident readers and strengthen the comprehension skills necessary for a lifetime of learning.

Each passage in *Nonfiction Reading Comprehension* covers a grade-level appropriate curriculum topic in geography, history, or science. The activities are time-efficient, allowing students to practice these skills often. To yield the best results, such practice must begin during the second quarter or when a solid majority of your class can read independently at a sixth-grade level.

✤ Essential Comprehension Skills

The questions following each passage in *Nonfiction Reading Comprehension* appear in the same order and cover seven vital skills:

✧ Locating facts

Questions based on exactly what the text states: who, what, when, where, why, and how many

✧ Identifying sequence

Questions based on chronological order: what happened first, last, and in between

✧ Noting conditions

Questions that ask students to identify similarities and differences, as well as cause-and-effect relationships

✧ Understanding vocabulary in context

Questions based on the ability to infer word meaning from the syntax and semantics of the surrounding text, as well as the ability to recognize known synonyms and antonyms for a newly encountered word

✧ Making inferences

Questions that require students to evaluate, make decisions, and draw logical conclusions

✧ Integrating knowledge

Questions that ask readers to draw upon their visualization skills combined with prior knowledge (These questions reinforce the crucial skill of picturing the text.)

✧ Supporting answers

A short-answer question at the end of each passage that helps students to personalize knowledge, state an opinion, and support it.

Meeting Standards and Benchmarks

Every passage in *Nonfiction Reading Comprehension* and its comprehension questions cover one or more of these language arts standards:

Reading	Writing
• Makes and revises predictions about text	• Writes compound sentences
• Uses prior knowledge to understand new information presented in text	• Follows conventions of capitalization, spelling, and punctuation appropriate for grade level
• Visualizes what is read	• Uses adjectives, adverbs, and pronouns to make writing diverse and interesting
• Uses context clues to decode unknown words	• Adheres to grammatical and mechanical conventions in writing
• Monitors own reading and independently takes action to increase understanding (self-corrects, rereads, slows down if necessary)	• States an opinion and supports it in writing
• Understands the main idea of nonfiction text	
• Integrates new information into personal knowledge base	
• Draws conclusions and makes inferences about information in the text	
• Develops ideas, opinions, and personal responses to what is read	

At the top of each passage appears the specific McREL content area standard and benchmark. Used with permission from McREL (Copyright 2000 McREL, Mid-continent Research for Education and Learning. Telephone: 303-337-0990. Web site: www.mcrel.org)

✦ Readability

All of the passages have a 6.0–6.9 reading level based on the Flesch Kincaid Readability Formula. This formula, which is built into Microsoft Word, determines a readability level by calculating the number of words, syllables, and sentences. Although content area terms can be challenging, students can handle difficult words within the context given. The passages are presented in order of increasing difficulty within each content area.

✦ Preparing Students to Read Nonfiction Text

Prepare your students to read the passages in *Nonfiction Reading Comprehension* by daily reading aloud a short nonfiction selection from another source. Reading expository text aloud is critical to developing your students' ability to read it themselves. Since making predictions is a good way to help students to understand nonfiction, read the beginning of a passage, then stop and ask them to predict what might occur next. Do this at several points throughout your reading of the text. Talking about nonfiction concepts is also very important. Remember, however, that discussion can never replace reading aloud because people rarely speak using the vocabulary and complex sentence structures of written language.

How to Use This Book

If you have some students who cannot read the articles independently, allow them to read with a partner, then work through the comprehension questions alone. As soon as possible, move to having all students practice reading and answering the questions independently.

✤ Multiple-Choice Questions

Do the first two passages and related questions on pages 8–11 with the whole class. These passages have the most challenging reading level because you will do them together. Demonstrate your own cognitive processes by thinking aloud about how to figure out an answer. This means that you tell your students your thoughts as they come to you. Let's say that this is a passage your class has read:

> Years ago 100,000 grizzly bears lived in the United States. Now there are only about 1,000, not including those that live in Alaska. In 1975 a law was passed to keep people from hunting the bears or destroying their homes. So today there are many more bears than in 1975. Almost all of them live in Yellowstone National Park. Sometimes the bears leave the park and kill cows or sheep. Some people feel afraid. They want to be able to shoot any grizzly that leaves the park. But others say that the bear population is already too small. They do not want the law changed.

Following the reading, one of the questions is: "In Yellowstone National park, grizzly bears a) live in cages, b) can do tricks, c) get caught in traps, or d) wander freely." Tell the students all your thoughts as they occur to you: "Well, the article said that the bears sometimes leave the park, so they must not be in cages. So I'll eliminate that choice. They are wild bears, so I doubt that they do any tricks. That leaves me with the choices 'get caught in traps' or 'wander around.' Let me look back at the article and see what it says about traps." (Refer back to article.) "I don't see anything about traps in the passage. And I did see that there is a law to keep the bears safe. That means they're safe from traps, which are dangerous. So I'm going to select 'd) wander around.'"

The fourth question is about vocabulary. Teach students to substitute the word choices for the vocabulary term (bolded) in the passage. For each choice they should ask, "Does this make sense?" This will help them to identify the best choice.

Teach students to look for the key words in a response or question and search for those specific words in the text. Explain that they may need to look for synonyms for the key words. When you go over the practice passages, ask your students to show where they found the correct response in the text.

How to Use This Book (cont.)

✤ Short-Answer Questions

The short-answer question for each passage is an opinion statement with no definitive right answer. Each student makes a statement and explains it. While there is no correct response, it is critical to show them how to support their opinions using facts and logic. Show them a format for response: reword the question as a statement that includes their opinion followed by the word "because" and a reason. Here's a good student response: "I do not think that whales should be kept at sea parks because they are wild animals. They want to be in the ocean with their herd. It's wrong to take animals from their native habitats and train them to do tricks for our enjoyment."

Do not award credit unless the student adequately supports his or her conclusion. Before passing back the practice papers, make note of two students with opposing opinions. Then, during the discussion, call on each of these students to read his or her short-answer response to the class. If all your students drew the same conclusion or had the same opinion, come up with support for the opposing one yourself.

For the most effective practice sessions, follow these six steps:

1. Have students read the text silently and answer the questions.

2. Collect all the papers to score them.

3. Return the papers to the students and discuss how they determined their answers.

4. Point out how students had to use their background knowledge to answer certain questions.

5. Call on at least two students with different viewpoints to read and discuss their responses to the short-answer question.

6. Have your students complete the achievement bar graph on page 7, showing how many questions they answered correctly for each practice passage. Seeing their scores improve or stay consistently high over time will provide encouragement and motivation.

Scoring the Passages

Since the passages are meant as skill builders, do not include the passage scores in students' class grades. With the students, use the "number correct" approach to scoring the practice passages, especially since this coincides with the student achievement graph. However, for your own records and to share with the parents, you may want to keep a track of numeric scores for each student. If you choose to do this, do not write the numeric score on the paper. To generate a numeric score, follow these guidelines:

Multiple Choice (6)	15 points each	90 points
Short Answer (1)	10 points	10 points
Total		**100 points**

✤ Practice Makes Perfect

The more your students practice, the more competent and confident they will become. Plan to have your class do every exercise in *Nonfiction Reading Comprehension*. If you do so, you'll be pleased with your students' improved comprehension of any expository text—within your classroom and beyond its walls.

Achievement Graph

Number Correct

Passage	1	2	3	4	5	6	7
"The Battle Against Germs"							
"Volatile Volcanoes"							
"The Father of Genetics"							
"Why Do Animals Act the Way They Do?"							
"The Water Cycle"							
"Your Remarkable Body"							
"Sun Storms"							
"Diamonds: The Gems from Deep in the Earth"							
"Brr! The Ice Ages"							
"Look Out for Lightning!"							
"Fire Fuels the Cycle of Life"							
"The Census Counts"							
"Terrifying Tsunamis"							
"Lake Erie's Struggle to Survive"							
"The California Gold Rush"							
"The Battle of Midway"							
"The Berlin Wall"							
"Let There be Light!"							
"Satellites"							
"Mexico: Past and Present"							

Science Standard: Knows the general structure and functions of cells in organisms

Benchmark: Knows that disease in organisms can be caused by intrinsic failures of the system or infection by another organism

The Battle Against Germs

Bacteria and viruses cause a lot of suffering for both people and animals. Many bacteria are dangerous. They eat living cells and produce poisons. Fortunately, we now have antibiotics to fight many of them. In 1928 Alexander Fleming worked in a lab in England. One day he found mold spreading through a dish of bacteria. It was dissolving the bacteria! Fleming had just discovered the first antibiotic, a mold called penicillin. Penicillin works because bacteria are living cells. Penicillin breaks the bacteria's cell wall. The material flows out of the cell, killing it.

No one in Europe showed interest in what Fleming had found! So Dr. Ernst Chain and Professor Howard Florey brought the information to America. The American government saw the value of penicillin and began to make it. At first the American government only let injured soldiers have the miracle drug. It kept them from dying from infected wounds. Then in 1943 a father begged for his dying two-year-old daughter to have the drug. After she received the medicine, she quickly recovered. From then on antibiotics were available to the public.

You have probably had a bad cold. You coughed a lot, your nose ran, and your head hurt. Bacteria did not cause your cold. A virus causes most colds. In fact, colds are the most common viruses. Unlike bacteria, a virus is not alive. Yet once it gets into your body, it takes over your living cells and reproduces rapidly. This makes you sick. With most viruses, your body's white blood cells will fight it off. You will get better within two weeks. However, some viruses, such as AIDS, can kill you. Today we have vaccines to keep us safe from many deadly viruses.

A vaccine can only work against a certain virus. That's why you must get a separate shot for each virus—such as polio or hepatitis. A vaccine can only protect you from a virus. It cannot fight bacteria. Bacteria are alive and can change over time. When bacteria change, they can become **resistant** to an antibiotic that once killed them. That medicine can no longer kill the germs. Doctors must take care not to give out antibiotics unless they are necessary.

The Battle Against Germs *(cont.)*

Comprehension Questions

1. **Antibiotics work against most**

   (a) bacteria.

   (b) viruses.

   (c) bacteria and viruses.

   (d) vaccines.

2. **On a historical timeline, what happened second?**

   (a) Fleming got excited about penicillin.

   (b) Chain and Florey promoted penicillin.

   (c) Most Europeans were not impressed by penicillin.

   (d) The American government made penicillin.

3. **How does an antibiotic differ from a vaccine?**

   (a) Vaccines fight bacterial infections; antibiotics fight viral infections.

   (b) Vaccines work for bacteria only; antibiotics work for both bacteria and viruses.

   (c) Each vaccine stops a specific virus; antibiotics work on many kinds of bacteria.

   (d) Vaccines are given after you get sick; antibiotics work before you get sick.

4. *Resistant* **means**

   (a) friendly.

   (b) unfriendly.

   (c) interference.

   (d) able to fight or oppose.

5. **Why do you think the Europeans showed so little interest in Fleming's finding?**

   (a) They probably thought it was too good to be true.

   (b) They probably thought that the mold looked too gross.

   (c) They probably didn't want to pay the high price Fleming demanded for penicillin.

   (d) They probably wanted someone else to try it out first.

6. **Picture Alexander Fleming's lab when he discovers penicillin. What don't you see?**

   (a) test tubes

   (b) a computer

   (c) bottle of chemicals

   (d) charts of data

7. **What disease would you most like to see a vaccine for? Explain.**

   _____

   _____

   _____

Geography Standard: Knows the physical processes that shape patterns on Earth's surface

Benchmark: Knows the consequences of a specific physical process operating on Earth's surface

Volatile Volcanoes

Volcanoes happen along the cracks between the Earth's plates. When a volcano erupts, melted rock from deep within the Earth spills out as lava. A volcano also releases solid rocks, ashes, and gases.

Since gases come from a volcano before, during, and after eruptions, scientists consider a volcano active as long as it **emits** gases. As liquid rock rises from the Earth's mantle, the gases and ashes separate from it. They form hot clouds that rise miles into the sky and glow at night. Although volcanic gas is mostly water vapor, it also has toxic gases. Fortunately, most of the gas goes so high into the air that it causes no harm. However, if the gases cause acid rain to fall, plants can die, sometimes hundreds of miles away.

Volcanoes erupt daily on the Pacific Ocean floor. The Hawaiian Islands sit atop a set of undersea volcanoes. After years of eruptions, the lava built up until the volcanoes reached the surface of the water. They emerged as islands. Every day new land is formed in Hawaii from the lava that continues to flow.

Land volcanoes do not erupt often. When they do, big chunks of rock called volcanic bombs may get thrown into the air. A river of lava may flow downhill, sometimes for miles. Although it usually only travels about three feet (1 m) an hour, it may move up to 25 miles per hour (40 kph). If a volcano erupts with great force, it can cause a mudflow. This means that rocks and soil from the sides of the volcano flow downhill like a river, destroying everything in their path. Mudflows often race down stream beds at speeds of up to 27 miles per hour (43 kph).

Sometimes volcanoes show up in odd places. After a series of earthquakes in February of 1943, a Mexican farmer saw steam rising from his cornfield. The next day the field had a wide crack. Ashes and gas shot out of the crack. To his surprise, he saw that a volcano was erupting right in the middle of his field! During the next nine years, its cone rose to 1,345 feet (300 m). Ashes covered the area, and several nearby towns lay buried beneath 100 feet (30 m) of lava. Then, just as suddenly as it started, it stopped.

With six billion people living on Earth, many live in the shadow of an active volcano. No one knows when volcanoes will erupt, and scientists always seek better ways to tell when they will happen. They want to give people enough warning to escape these natural disasters.

Volatile Volcanoes (cont.)

Comprehension Questions

1. No one can tell

  (a) which volcanoes are active.

  (b) where volcanoes are located on the ocean floor.

  (c) when a specific volcano will erupt.

  (d) if a volcano is extinct.

2. With the 1943 Mexican volcano, what happened third?

  (a) Gas and ashes spewed out on the cornfield.

  (b) A big crack developed in the cornfield.

  (c) Earthquakes shook a farm.

  (d) Steam rose from the cornfield.

3. Why does a mudflow usually gush down a stream or river?

  (a) because there's little in the way to stop it

  (b) because it's less dangerous

  (c) because the mud is attracted to the water

  (d) because people set up sandbags to direct the mudflow into the waterway

4. Another word for *emits* is

  (a) holds.   (c) destroys.

  (b) collects.   (d) releases.

5. What natural disaster often occurs along with a volcano?

  (a) a tornado   (c) a landslide

  (b) a flood   (d) a hurricane

6. Picture a volcanic eruption. If people are trapped nearby, what vehicle has the best chance of rescuing them?

  (a) a tank   (c) a helicopter

  (b) a jet   (d) a four-wheel-drive truck

7. Should there be laws keeping people from building anywhere near an active volcano? Explain.

_____

_____

_____

Science Standard: Understands the scientific enterprise

Benchmark: Knows that throughout history, many scientific innovators have had difficulty breaking through accepted ideas of their time to reach conclusions that are now considered common knowledge

The Father of Genetics

In 1822 Gregor Mendel was born on a farm in Austria. His father encouraged Mendel's fascination with plants. He knew that his son was intelligent, and he wanted him to have a good education. So he sent Mendel to high school. At that time few people attended high school, and those who did lived there. However, since his father could not pay the full **tuition,** Mendel received no food. He always felt hungry, but he survived because the other students gave him the scraps from their plates.

As an adult Mendel became a monk and continued his studies. He tended the gardens at the monastery where he and the other monks lived. He did experiments with pea plants for eight years. He wanted to prove that parents passed characteristics to their offspring. Over time he found that plants have genes. Genes carry codes for features from one generation to the next. Around 1860 Mendel discovered recessive and dominant genes. Dominant genes showed up the most often in offspring. Recessive genes only showed up occasionally and only when both parents carried the gene for the trait.

How did he figure this out? He bred a tall pea plant with a short pea plant. Every one of the first generation of four pea plants was tall. This meant that tall was the dominant gene. Yet in the next generation of four pea plants, one plant was very short. The recessive short genes it received from both of its parent plants had made it short.

Eager to share his finding with others, he wrote a paper. No one paid any attention to it. During his lifetime no one cared about what he had discovered. At the time of his death, he still felt frustrated because his knowledge went unrecognized.

Finally, his important discovery was recognized in 1990. We now know that both plants and animals have genes and that genes play a major role in how we look, how we act, and whether or not we are apt to get certain diseases. Today, Gregor Mendel is called the "Father of Genetics."

The Father of Genetics *(cont.)*

Comprehension Questions

1. **Scientists acknowledged Mendel's discovery about genetics worldwide**

   ⓐ before his death.

   ⓑ more than 100 years after he figured it out.

   ⓒ during the 19th century.

   ⓓ just last year.

2. **On a historical timeline, what happened second?**

   ⓐ Mendel learned how parents pass genes to offspring.

   ⓑ Mendel became a monk.

   ⓒ Mendel conducted extensive plant experiments.

   ⓓ Mendel wrote a paper to share his discoveries.

3. **Mendel found out that when both parents carry a recessive gene,**

   ⓐ there is a strong chance that their child will inherit the trait.

   ⓑ there is some chance that their child will inherit the trait.

   ⓒ there is no chance that their child will inherit the trait.

   ⓓ their child will definitely inherit the trait.

4. **Which is an example of *tuition*?**

   ⓐ finishing a school project on time

   ⓑ knowing something is going to happen before it happens

   ⓒ buying food in a restaurant

   ⓓ spending money on school courses

5. **How do you think Mendel felt about the students who gave him their scraps?**

   ⓐ overjoyed   ⓒ grateful

   ⓑ annoyed   ⓓ disgusted

6. **Picture Mendel writing the paper about his findings. What is he using?**

   ⓐ a quill pen   ⓒ a ball-point pen

   ⓑ a word processor   ⓓ a marker

7. **Should scientists continue to study genetics? Explain.**

   _____

   _____

   _____

Science Standard: Understands the genetic basis for the transfer of biological characteristics from one generation to the next

Benchmark: Knows that the characteristics of an organism can be described in terms of a combination of traits; some traits are inherited and others result from interactions with the environment

Why Do Animals Act the Way They Do?

All animal behavior comes from instincts, learning, or reasoning. Instinctive behavior comes from reflexes and the urge to survive and reproduce. Every newborn has reflexes. Reflexes happen automatically, without conscious thought. If you pick up something that's very hot, you will immediately drop it. You don't have to think about it, and no one has to tell you to do it. In fact, the pain message doesn't even make it to your brain before you react. Your spinal cord triggers your reflex reaction to pain.

Every animal wants to stay alive. When an animal feels fear, it fights or flees. Depending on the enemy, the animal will fight or run away. To protect her pups, a mother walrus will attack a polar bear. A squirrel will run up a tree to **elude** a fox.

Species would die off without the urge to reproduce. This instinct causes animals to mate. Some animals, like birds, also have an instinct to care for their young. Birds sit on their eggs until they hatch. They bring food to the babies, and they chase away predators that approach the nest. Mammals take care of their young, too.

Unlike instincts, learning comes from experience. Learning helps a species to survive. For example, if a heron finds a good spot to catch frogs, it will repeatedly return to the same place. Animals learn through imitation, too. Birds learn to fly by watching their parents. Lions and other predators teach their babies how to hunt for food.

All animals have instincts and many animals can learn, but few can reason. Animals that can reason can think about what to do the first time they encounter a situation. A seeing-eye dog knows how to guide a blind person safely down a sidewalk, but it must use reason to figure out what to do in a new, unusual situation. For example, the dog must decide what to do when it comes to a car that's completely blocking the sidewalk. So far, scientists have discovered that humans, dogs, chimpanzees, porpoises, and dolphins can reason.

Why Do Animals Act the Way They Do? *(cont.)*

Comprehension Questions

1. **Which animal can reason?**

   ⓐ cats

   ⓑ herons

   ⓒ lions

   ⓓ dolphins

2. **Read all of the statements. Decide what happens third.**

   ⓐ The polar bear goes away.

   ⓑ The polar bear tries to snatch the infant.

   ⓒ The mother walrus attacks the polar bear with her tusks.

   ⓓ A polar bear sees a baby walrus.

3. **What's an example of a human reflex?**

   ⓐ giggling

   ⓑ sneezing

   ⓒ scratching

   ⓓ sleeping

4. **A synonym for *elude* is**

   ⓐ escape.

   ⓑ attack.

   ⓒ trick.

   ⓓ scare.

5. **Based on the animals that we know can reason, which of these animals can also probably reason?**

   ⓐ opossums

   ⓑ wolves

   ⓒ squirrels

   ⓓ barracudas

6. **Picture an animal wandering into traffic on a busy street. What is the animal most apt to do?**

   ⓐ leap up on a car

   ⓑ sit still and hope the cars don't hit it

   ⓒ run away from the cars

   ⓓ play dead by laying flat in the road

7. **Since it's against the urge to survive, why do you think that whales sometimes beach themselves? Explain.**

   _____

   _____

   _____

Science Standard: Understands basic features of the Earth

Benchmark: Knows the processes involved in the water cycle

The Water Cycle

Our Earth is a closed system. All of its elements are already here. More elements do not enter into it. This means that all the water that ever was here is still here. How can that be? Because our Earth recycles its elements, using each one over and over again.

Every drop of water on the Earth has gone through the water cycle. Much of it has gone through the cycle billions of times. All of the water on Earth is always in some stage of the water cycle. The water is either in storage, evaporation, condensation, precipitation, percolation, or runoff. All of the ice frozen in glaciers and all of the water in oceans,

lakes, rivers, and underground aquifers is in the storage stage. During the evaporation stage, liquid water changes to vapor. This vapor enters the atmosphere. When the vapor cools, it condenses and forms clouds. Later the clouds drop precipitation in the form of rain or snow, and the water falls back to the ground. Much of this precipitation seeps down through the ground in a process called percolation. The rest runs into streams, lakes, rivers, and oceans. Such runoff increases during storms, rainy seasons, and after snow and ice melt.

Humans have affected the water cycle for thousands of years. We dig ditches to bring water to dry land. We build dams to control flooding and provide electrical power. We drill wells to pump up groundwater. In some areas of the U.S. people have drained underground aquifers that took thousands of years to fill. As a result, the ground may begin to cave in.

The oceans hold about 97 percent of all the water on Earth. Since sea water is salty, we cannot drink it. However, if water evaporates from an ocean, it leaves its salt behind. So when it falls as precipitation, it's fresh water. The fresh water in glaciers stays frozen for hundreds of years. Thus, we cannot easily **access** this water. Most groundwater is found in the first ten miles of the Earth's crust, and we can tap this supply. Water below this depth can only return to the Earth's surface during a volcanic eruption.

The Water Cycle *(cont.)*

Comprehension Questions

1. **Steam is in what stage of the water cycle?**

   (a) condensation (c) evaporation

   (b) percolation (d) precipitation

2. **Read all of the statements. Decide what happened third.**

   (a) An aquifer was drained.

   (b) People pumped out water.

   (c) Many people drilled wells.

   (d) A ground depression (sinkhole) formed.

3. **Water stays the longest time in which stage of the water cycle?**

   (a) evaporation (c) precipitation

   (b) storage (d) condensation

4. **Another word for *access* is**

   (a) drink. (c) obtain.

   (b) buy. (d) freeze.

5. **How does an aquifer fill with water?**

   (a) Rainwater percolates until it reaches the aquifer.

   (b) The aquifer absorbs clouds.

   (c) Ocean floods fill the aquifer.

   (d) People pump water into the aquifer.

6. **Picture a foggy day. The fog means that water is in which two stages of the water cycle?**

   (a) storage and condensation

   (b) percolation and runoff

   (c) evaporation and precipitation

   (d) precipitation and condensation

7. **Should we satisfy a growing need for more fresh water by melting polar ice? Explain.**

   _____

   _____

   _____

Science Standard: Knows the general structure and functions of cells in organisms

Benchmark: Knows that multicellular organisms have a variety of specialized cells, tissues, organs, and organ systems that perform specialized functions

Your Remarkable Body

Your body is a remarkable machine. Just as a machine's many parts work together to make it run, your body's systems work together to keep you alive. These include the endocrine, skin, and nervous systems.

Your endocrine system has the glands that make saliva and stomach acid, sweat, and tears. The endocrine glands produce chemicals called hormones. The blood carries these hormones through the body. When a hormone reaches the right organs or tissues, it causes things to happen. For example, after a meal the hormone insulin tells cells to take sugar out of the blood. The most important part of this system is the pituitary gland. This gland sends out the hormones that control all of the other endocrine glands.

The skin is your body's largest organ. Skin has three layers. The top layer keeps germs, chemicals, and the sun's harmful rays away from your internal organs. Nerves in the middle layer of skin react to heat, cold, pain, pressure, and touch. When you feel too cold, the blood vessels in this layer get smaller to stop heat loss. This can cause goosebumps. When you feel too hot, these blood vessels get bigger to let heat escape. The sweat glands in the middle layer of the skin produce sweat. As the sweat evaporates, it cools the body. The bottom skin layer has fat cells. This fat layer helps the body stay warm and cushions the inner body tissues against **impacts** (such as when you fall down or get hit by a moving object).

Since the nervous system controls every other body system, it is the most complex system. It has millions of nerve cells in every part of the body. The nervous system has three parts: the autonomic nervous system, the central nervous system (your brain and spinal cord), and your sensory organs. The autonomic nervous system keeps the body's automatic functions working constantly. It keeps your heart beating and lungs breathing even while you sleep. The spinal cord and the brain get information and decide how the body should respond. The spinal cord controls your pain reflexes, such as dropping a match when it burns your finger. Most decisions, however, use the brain. The brain works at the conscious level when you control a decision. You can decide whether or not to scratch your arm. When you have no control over the decision, your brain works at the subconscious level. If your brain decides that you need to sneeze, you will. You can't help it.

Each of your sensory organs sends nerve signals to your brain. Your eyes change light waves into nerve signals, just as your ears change sound waves into nerve signals. When these messages make the central nervous believe that action is necessary, it sends out the instructions to make the action occur.

Your Remarkable Body (cont.)

Comprehension Questions

1. **The biggest organ in the human body is**

   (a) the skin.

   (b) the spinal cord.

   (c) the brain.

   (d) the autonomic nervous system.

2. **Read all of the statements. Decide what happens second.**

   (a) You throw your hands over your face.

   (b) A baseball flies at your face.

   (c) Your brain prompts you to instantly respond.

   (d) Your spinal cord prompts you to instantly respond.

3. **You see a very sad movie. What body system brings tears to your eyes?**

   (a) the circulatory system

   (b) the autonomic nervous system

   (c) the endocrine system

   (d) the skin system

4. **An example of an *impact* is**

   (a) throwing a football.

   (c) sleeping on the ground.

   (b) walking into a wall.

   (d) eating a piece of pie.

5. **What body system causes you to shiver when you feel cold?**

   (a) the nervous system

   (c) the skin system

   (b) the endocrine system

   (d) the digestive system

6. **Picture a person eating a large meal. Which body system is most affected by this?**

   (a) the respiratory system

   (c) the skin system

   (b) the nervous system

   (d) the endocrine system

7. **Which body system do you think is the most interesting? Explain.**

   _____

   _____

   _____

Science Standard: Understands essential ideas about the composition and structure of the universe and Earth's place in it

Benchmark: Knows characteristics of our sun and its position in the universe

Sun Storms

You know that the sun **sustains** life here on Earth. You know that you should never look directly at the sun because it could blind you. But did you know that the sun has weather? Of course it's nothing like the weather on Earth. In comparison, our most powerful storm seems like a mild breeze. And believe it or not, what it's doing up there on the sun affects us down here!

Our sun is a huge ball of burning plasma—a state of matter where gas is superheated. Most of this plasma is hydrogen gas. The sun has an 11-year cycle. Throughout the cycle, the sun has periods of major storm activity and minor storm activity. During the major storm part of the cycle, the sun has lots of solar flares. Solar flares are plasma eruptions that shoot off the sun's surface, causing solar wind. Just one average-sized solar flare releases enough energy to meet all the current power needs of the U.S. for 10,000 years! The biggest solar flares extend out into space like gigantic clouds. These clouds move a million miles per hour (1,609,344 kph) toward Earth as solar wind.

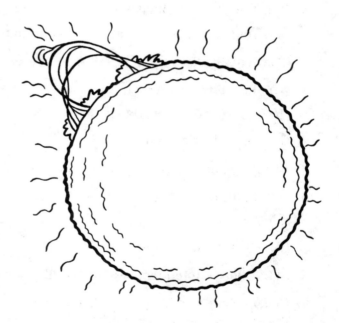

When strong solar winds hit Earth's atmosphere, the night sky glows with colored lights reflecting off the ice at the Earth's North Pole. People call them the Northern Lights.

Unfortunately, solar winds don't just provide interesting sky effects. They can cause harmful magnetic storms. These storms can disrupt phone, TV, and radio signals, the Internet, and e-mail. They can make radar systems crash. They can destroy satellites and kill astronauts working outside the space shuttle. The biggest threat comes from the magnetic storm's ability to knock out electrical power. This happened in 1989 when Quebec, a large region in Canada, lost its entire electrical power service grid in less than 90 seconds. The problem took so long to fix that many people had to go without heat or electricity for a month.

Sun Storms (cont.)

Comprehension Questions

1. **The Northern Lights are caused by**

   ⓐ magnetic storms.   ⓒ plasma.

   ⓑ solar wind.   ⓓ hydrogen gas.

2. **What happened second in 1989?**

   ⓐ The sun had one or more major plasma eruptions.

   ⓑ People went without electricity for a month.

   ⓒ Solar wind created a magnetic storm.

   ⓓ Quebec's power grid was heavily damaged.

3. **Even small solar flares cause some**

   ⓐ solar wind.   ⓒ Northern Lights.

   ⓑ plasma.   ⓓ hydrogen gas.

4. **An antonym for *sustains* is**

   ⓐ burns.   ⓒ maintains.

   ⓑ chills.   ⓓ destroys.

5. **What usually protects us from the harmful effects of solar wind?**

   ⓐ the Northern Lights

   ⓑ power grids

   ⓒ Earth's atmosphere

   ⓓ plasma eruptions

6. **Picture a team of scientists discovering a way to collect and use solar flare energy. What is the expression on their faces?**

   ⓐ excited   ⓒ annoyed

   ⓑ upset   ⓓ bored

7. **Do you think it's important for scientists to continue studying solar weather? Explain.**

   _____

   _____

   _____

Science Standard: Understands basic Earth processes

Benchmark: Knows processes involved in the rock cycle

Diamonds: The Gems from Deep in the Earth

Diamonds are the most valuable of gems and the hardest mineral. Yet every diamond starts out as just a chunk of carbon. Carbon is an element found in all living things. When leaves fall on the ground or animals die, they rot. Their carbon goes into the soil. During the rock cycle, the carbon gets buried below the Earth's surface. Over time, more and more rock layers form above it. In some places this carbon then changes into coal. If the carbon gets pushed very deep into the Earth's mantle, the high pressure and extreme heat cause it to change into diamond crystals. These crystals can split along lines. Diamonds can be cut in such a way as to sparkle when they reflect light. This is why people use them in jewelry.

Over thousands of years, earthquakes move these diamond crystals closer to the surface of the Earth. Others get brought up with the lava and ash of volcanic eruptions. South Africa and Australia have the most diamonds, but even in those places, they are rare. Usually a diamond mine must dig up and crush more than one ton (907 kg) of rock to get a single gem.

No acid can dissolve a diamond, and a diamond is so hard that only another diamond can cut it. Only very **intense** heat or a sharp blow can destroy a diamond. Because they are so durable, mining drill bits have diamond tips. Diamonds are also used to cut, grind, and shape hard materials. Every day manufacturers use diamonds to make parts for cars, planes, and engines.

However, there aren't enough natural diamonds to meet industry's needs. So scientists at General Electric figured out how to make diamonds. They did this by copying a part of the rock cycle. Using the same conditions as those present deep in the Earth, they put carbon under high heat and pressure until a diamond formed. Since these man-made diamonds cost even more than natural ones, only businesses buy them.

Diamonds: The Gems from Deep in the Earth *(cont.)*

Comprehension Questions

1. **Diamonds are a rare form of**

   (a) marble.

   (b) granite.

   (c) lava.

   (d) carbon.

2. **During the formation of a diamond, what happens third?**

   (a) The carbon crystallizes.

   (b) Volcanoes push the carbon closer to the Earth's surface.

   (c) Carbon gets compressed under great heat and weight.

   (d) Layers of rock form above carbon.

3. **Which of the following could destroy a diamond?**

   (a) pouring acid on the diamond

   (b) smashing the diamond with a hammer

   (c) leaving the diamond outside in bad weather

   (d) putting the diamond in direct sunlight on a hot day

4. *Intense* **means**

   (a) mild.

   (b) dry.

   (c) extreme.

   (d) humid.

5. **An example of carbon is**

   (a) coal.

   (b) water.

   (c) air.

   (d) sand.

6. **Picture a jewelry shop window filled with diamonds. Which item is the most expensive?**

   (a) the Australian diamond

   (b) the African diamond

   (c) the smallest diamond

   (d) the largest diamond

7. **Why do you think diamonds remain popular in jewelry despite their high cost? Explain.**

   _____

   _____

   _____

Geography Standard: Knows the physical processes that shape patterns on Earth's surface

Benchmark: Knows the major processes that shape patterns in the physical environment

Brrr! The Ice Ages

No one knows for sure what triggers an ice age. Most scientists believe that between every 10,000 to 20,000 years the Earth wobbles a little bit. This causes a slight change in its orbit around the sun. As a result, the area around the North Pole gets less sunlight. Then the ice sheets that cover the Arctic Circle start to spread south.

During an ice age, huge ice sheets called glaciers cover a lot of the Earth's land. The frozen water trapped in glaciers comes from the oceans. This makes the sea level drop all over the world. As the water level falls, land that used to be underwater gets revealed. Since water absorbs the sun's heat better than land, the reduction of ocean water substantially cools the Earth's atmosphere. This means that instead of a scorching 98°F (37°C) day, a really hot summer day would be just 71°F (22°C). Only near the equator do temperatures stay relatively normal during an ice age.

Glaciers **alter** the Earth's surface. The slow-moving ice sheets keep water from draining away, forming lakes. Rivers change their courses to flow along the edges of the ice. Rain or snow falls on the glaciers. That water freezes and adds to its weight. The heavy weight can push the Earth's crust down by as much as 1,000 feet (305 m). In fact, the continent of Antarctica is almost completely underwater because of the weight of its two-mile-thick glaciers!

The freezing and thawing of glaciers causes erosion of the rocks under and near the ice sheets. These loose rock pieces get dragged along, scratching deep grooves into the land. This can turn V-shaped mountain valleys into wider, deeper U-shaped valleys. As glacier ice melts, it drops pieces of rock and soil, forming a series of hills or ridges. During the time between ice ages, the ice sheets mostly disappear. Although we live in one of those times, huge, thick sheets of ice still cover much of Greenland and almost all of Antarctica.

The Earth has had several ice ages, and each one lasted for thousands of years. The last ice age ended about 11,500 years ago. Many scientists agree that a new ice age could begin at any time.

Brrr! The Ice Ages *(cont.)*

Comprehension Questions

1. **Glaciers often change**

   (a) the length of an ice age. (c) the temperature at the North Pole.

   (b) the Earth's orbit around the sun. (d) the course of rivers.

2. **During an ice age, what happens second?**

   (a) Glaciers extend further south than usual. (c) The level of the Earth's oceans falls.

   (b) The North Pole gets less sunlight. (d) The Earth's orbit changes slightly.

3. **A glacier moving across land is most like**

   (a) a whittling knife carving a chunk of wood.

   (b) a ship moving through big waves.

   (c) a chain saw cutting down a tree.

   (d) the damage caused by a tornado.

4. ***Alter* means**

   (a) damage. (c) change.

   (b) cool. (d) create.

5. **What effect would global warming most likely have on glaciers?**

   (a) Glaciers might float to cooler places.

   (b) More glaciers would form.

   (c) Glaciers would start to form in Africa.

   (d) Glaciers might melt.

6. **Picture a V-shaped mountain valley. Do you think a glacier formed it?**

   (a) No, because the valley would be more U-shaped if it'd been formed by a glacier.

   (b) No, because glaciers never affect valleys.

   (c) Yes, glaciers have made all the valleys on Earth.

   (d) Yes, glaciers often left this type of valley as they retreated.

7. **Do you think it would be difficult for the people in this country to survive an ice age? Explain.**

   _____

   _____

   _____

Geography Standard: Understands how physical systems affect human systems

Benchmark: Knows ways in which people prepare for natural hazards

Look Out for Lightning!

Lightning, one of nature's most powerful forces, can kill people and animals, destroy buildings and trees, and start raging forest fires. While lightning usually comes with a thunderstorm, it can also occur during snowstorms, sandstorms, and in the clouds of a volcanic eruption. Every second, approximately 100 lightning bolts strike the Earth. Areas closest to the Equator get the most strikes.

Lightning keeps the electrical balance in clouds. Everything has tiny particles called electrons and protons. Lightning occurs when the electrons move toward protons. The electrons jump at high speed to protons within the same cloud, another cloud, or on the ground. When the electrons move, the air gets so hot that its temperature exceeds that of the sun's surface. The air glows, and the burst of extreme heat makes the moist air explode, causing the sound waves we call thunder. That's why the clap of thunder always follows a lightning flash.

You have probably seen jagged lightning bolts streaking from the sky toward the ground. When these clouds-to-ground lightning bolts strike a beach, they melt the sand into fulgurite, a type of glass. But usually these kinds of bolts hit the tallest thing in the area. In fact, the Empire State Building in New York City gets struck by lightning an average of 23 times each year. The people who design skyscrapers know this. So skyscrapers have systems to keep lightning strikes from causing damage.

No one knows exactly when or where lightning will strike, but we do know that we should take steps to avoid getting hit by lightning. If you can, go inside at the first sign of lightning. It's much safer indoors. However, lightning can still reach into a building, so don't talk on the phone or stand at a window. Do not swim if there is lightning in the area. If you are out in a boat, get down inside the cabin. If you are caught outside away from buildings, get into a car or a truck. Never take shelter under a tree. Trees can get struck by lightning, and the electricity would move through them to you.

Even though lightning is **hazardous**, it is essential for our planet. Every bolt produces ozone gas. The ozone gas in our atmosphere protects us from the sun's strong radiation. Each lightning bolt also cleans the air by making pieces of pollution fall to the ground.

Look Out for Lightning! *(cont.)*

Comprehension Questions

1. Fulgurite is

   (a) a device for measuring the intensity of lightning bolts.

   (b) a type of glass made by lightning.

   (c) the area that lightning strikes most frequently.

   (d) a kind of lightning.

2. During a lightning strike, what happens third?

   (a) The air glows brightly.   (c) Air expanding causes a clap of thunder.

   (b) The air gets incredibly hot.   (d) Electrons race toward protons.

3. A lightning strike is most apt to cause

   (a) a vehicle fire.   (c) a forest fire.

   (b) a skyscraper fire.   (d) a factory fire.

4. A synonym for *hazardous* is

   (a) dangerous.   (c) loud.

   (b) hot.   (d) electrical.

5. How would going into a small boat's cabin help you to survive a thunderstorm?

   (a) You could fight a fire caused by the lightning better from within the boat's cabin.

   (b) A lightning bolt cannot reach inside boat cabins.

   (c) A lightning bolt that could enter a boat cabin would be weaker than most.

   (d) A lighting bolt wouldn't directly strike you as it might if you were on the boat's deck.

6. Picture watching a summer thunderstorm rapidly approach a small ocean harbor. What won't you see?

   (a) a few boats hurrying toward shore

   (b) small pleasure boats leaving the dock to go out to sea

   (c) swimmers getting out of the water

   (d) dark clouds

7. When a lightning storm approaches your area, should network TV stations run warnings during regular programming? Explain.

_____

_____

_____

Geography Standard: Understands the characteristics of ecosystems on Earth's surface

Benchmark: Understands the functions and dynamics of ecosystems

Fire Fuels the Cycle of Life

True or false: Forest fires can be good for an ecosystem. Think it's false? No, it's true! Forests actually need fires to release the minerals stored within dead and living plants and trees. Fires keep the forest from taking over the meadows that border it. After a large fire, these fields grow rapidly because of the nutrients set free by the blaze. Forest fires make new habitats, encouraging greater plant and animal variety. The greatest number of different species is found about 25 years after a major blaze.

In 1972 when scientists found out that fires were helpful, national parks adopted a new policy: No one would fight any fire started by a lightning strike. Most fires caused by lightning would go out by themselves in a few hours. This would result in **minimal** damage while allowing natural and necessary blazes.

However, during the summer of 1988, Yellowstone National Park had a serious drought. No rain fell. Old, dead pine trees lay stacked on the forest floor like logs in a fireplace. On June 14 lightning started a fire. Due to the policy, it was left to burn. When it still hadn't gone out on its own after five weeks, things looked grim. Finally, people started fighting the fire. By then the situation was completely out of control. The fire raged all summer, stopping only when snow fell in September. The gigantic blaze had destroyed almost half of the Park, burning about a million acres (405,000 hectacres). It seemed like a big disaster.

Yet in a forest the cycle of life is based on fire. Just one year after Yellowstone's huge fire, its forest showed new growth. Its most plentiful trees, lodgepole pines, have cones that actually need the high temperatures of a fire to open and drop their seeds. Their tiny saplings poked up through the charred soil. A flowering plant called fireweed blanketed the area.

After another 200 years, Yellowstone will burn again, and the cycle will start over.

Fire Fuels the Cycle of Life! *(cont.)*

Comprehension Questions

1. How is a forest fire beneficial?

(a) It gives firefighters jobs.

(b) It releases trapped nutrients from plants and trees.

(c) It gives scientists a chance to study forest fires.

(d) It attracts lightning strikes away from people's homes.

2. What happened second during the summer of 1988?

(a) People did not respond immediately.

(b) Lightning caused a forest fire in Yellowstone National Park.

(c) The fire was stopped by snowfall.

(d) New habitats formed.

3. The 1988 drought caused Yellowstone National Park to

(a) be cooler than normal.

(b) support greater plant and animal variety.

(c) have very dry conditions.

(d) attract more lightning strikes than usual.

4. An antonym for *minimal* is

(a) costly.   (b) much.   (c) little.   (d) limited.

5. Based on Yellowstone's forest fire cycle, prior to 1988, when had its last major blaze occurred?

(a) around 1588   (c) around 1788

(b) around 1688   (d) around 1888

6. Picture Yellowstone in October of 1988. What do you see?

(a) Firefighters are spraying water on a huge forest fire.

(b) Most of the trees have colored leaves, and colored leaves blanket the ground.

(c) Tiny pine trees and flowering fireweed are everywhere you look.

(d) There's snow on the ground, and few standing trees are black and bare.

7. Do you agree with the policy of allowing fires started by lightning to burn themselves out? Explain.

_____

_____

_____

Geography Standard: Understands the nature, distribution, and migration of human populations on Earth's surface

Benchmark: Understands demographic concepts and how they are used to describe population characteristics of a country or region

The Census Counts

Starting with the first census in 1790, the U.S. has had a census every ten years. The census counts every person living in the U.S. on a certain date. It also includes American citizens, such as soldiers, living abroad. The census data gives useful **statistics**. It tells where Americans live and the size of their families. It tells how many people have come from other places. It shows the number of people in each age group. The census finds out what people do for a living, how much money they earn, and how much education they have. It reports the number of births, deaths, marriages, and divorces. Although the census asks personal information, no names are attached to the public data. No one can find out another's private information—like age or salary.

The Constitution requires a census once a decade to decide how many people each state should have in the House of Representatives. The states with the biggest population send the most people to Congress. States with fewer people do not send as many. After a census, some states may gain seats in the House of Representatives. Other states may lose seats. Based on the 2000 census data, New York State lost two seats.

The government needs the census data for other reasons, too. They look to see if the population is growing. They can tell if it is increasing in some areas and decreasing in others. By looking at the age groups, they can see if people are living longer. They can figure out average life expectancy (how long a person usually lives). By looking at the number of births, it's possible to predict the number of babies to expect in the near future. If the number of children is rising, there may be a need for more schools and teachers.

Census data helps the government and businesses decide where to spend money. Census numbers determine how federal funds get spent on housing, schools, and welfare. Companies can use census data to choose where to build a new factory. They want to put it in an area with many workers. Stores want to be near plenty of shoppers.

Today, nearly 90 percent of the world's countries do a population census. The U.S. collects the most detailed data of all. The 2000 census resulted in over half a million pages of information.

The Census Counts (cont.)

Comprehension Questions

1. **The U.S.A. takes a census once every**

   (a) year.   (b) five years.   (c) decade.   (d) century.

2. **On a historical timeline, what happens last?**

   (a) Every person in the U.S.A. must respond to the census questions.

   (b) The government takes a census.

   (c) Businesses make informed decisions.

   (d) The government publishes the data it gathered.

3. **A group of pediatricians examines the census data to help decide in which state they should set up their practice. What information would most interest these doctors?**

   (a) the education level of people in each state

   (b) the number of divorces in each state

   (c) the average income of the people living in each state

   (d) the number of children living in each state

4. ***Statistics* are**

   (a) pieces of information; often numerical facts.   (c) tips about the stock market.

   (b) government budgets.   (d) estimated information.

5. **Which of these questions would not be asked on the U.S. census?**

   (a) What is your occupation?   (c) Where were you born?

   (b) What do you weigh?   (d) What is your marital status?

6. **Picture the pages stored on the CD-ROM that the U.S. government creates to make the census results public. What do you see on the pages?**

   (a) private information about each specific person in the U.S.

   (b) mostly photographs

   (c) mathematical formulas

   (d) graphs and charts showing data

7. **Do you think that the census should be taken more often? Explain.**

   _____

   _____

   _____

Geography Standard: Knows the physical processes that shape patterns on Earth's surface

Benchmark: Knows the consequences of a specific physical process operating on Earth's surface

Terrifying Tsunamis

Tsunamis, also called tidal waves, are giant ocean waves caused by an undersea earthquake or a major volcanic eruption. Either event can cause a sudden change to the ocean floor that jolts the water above. The resulting tidal wave races across the ocean at speeds of up to 500 miles per hour (805 kph). If you were in a nearby ship at sea, you probably would not even notice the wave because the water is so deep. However, the water near the shore is shallow. The water slows down, building up to an enormous height. When a tidal wave hits shore, it may tower more than 100 feet (30 m) high. That's taller than a ten-story building! Even worse, more waves may arrive a few minutes or hours after the first. These waves break on coasts hundreds or even thousands of miles away from where the earthquake or volcano occurred. Most tsunamis occur in the Pacific Ocean.

Tidal waves are one of the most deadly natural disasters. They can destroy all life and property wherever they hit. In 1883 a volcano caused a tsunami to wipe out the islands of Java and Sumatra. Over 36,000 people died. Only one person survived. Fortunately today scientists can often figure out when and where a tidal wave will reach shore. They advise people to leave those areas. However, sometimes the warning does not come in time.

Some people confuse storm surges with tidal waves. While they share similarities, a storm surge comes with a hurricane. During a hurricane, strong winds whip the ocean into huge waves. The first big waves reach land when the center of the storm is about 100 miles (161 km) offshore. When the storm itself hits the shore, the bulge of water directly under the eye of the storm smashes into the coast, gushing up to a mile inland. You don't want to be anywhere nearby when that happens! Even if you did not drown, when the water **recedes**, it drags things such as cars and houses out to sea. The worst storm surge to ever strike America happened when a hurricane struck Galveston, Texas in 1900. Over 8,000 people died.

Terrifying Tsunamis *(cont.)*

Comprehension Questions

1. **What other natural disaster do people confuse with tsunamis?**

   ⓐ storm surges   ⓒ hurricanes

   ⓑ tidal waves   ⓓ earthquakes

2. **During a storm surge, what happens second?**

   ⓐ Large objects get carried out into the ocean.

   ⓑ A huge mound of water slams into shore.

   ⓒ Large waves pound the coast.

   ⓓ A hurricane forms.

3. **Where's the safest place to be in a tsunami?**

   ⓐ in a sea cave on the coast

   ⓑ on a ship in the harbor

   ⓒ in a house at the seashore

   ⓓ on a ship near the place where the tsunami starts

4. ***Recedes* means**

   ⓐ pushes ahead.   ⓒ increases.

   ⓑ moves back.   ⓓ rises.

5. **Which place is most apt to experience a tsunami?**

   ⓐ New Jersey   ⓒ Africa

   ⓑ Alaska   ⓓ England

6. **Picture a Hawaiian community warned of a tsunami that will strike within an hour. What are most of the people doing?**

   ⓐ going to the coast to watch the tsunami come in

   ⓑ nailing boards over the windows of their homes

   ⓒ getting into a sailboat and sailing out to sea

   ⓓ hurrying to move inland

7. **Should laws prevent people from living on any shore that's ever experienced a tsunami? Explain.**

   _____

   _____

   _____

Geography Standard: Understands the characteristics of ecosystems on Earth's surface

Benchmark: Understands ecosystems in terms of their ability to withstand stress caused by physical events

Lake Erie's Struggle to Survive

America and Canada share an important natural resource called the Great Lakes. These five lakes hold one-fifth of the world's fresh water. They are so large that they can be seen from outer space. As the warmest and shallowest of the Great Lakes, Lake Erie's average depth is just 62 feet (19 meters).

From the mid-1800s to the mid-1900s, cities and farms dumped untreated waste right into the lake. The people believed that the lake was so big that all of the waste and chemicals would be **diluted** into insignificance. Although all of the Great Lakes suffered from pollution, Lake Erie received the most damage due to its warm temperature and shallow depth. By the late 1960s, the lake was so foul that most of its fish had died. The high bacteria count made the water unsafe for swimming. The lake stunk from algae overgrowth. On its surface floated mats of green slime. Its condition was so bad that scientists called Lake Erie "dead."

In 1972 the Canadian and American governments agreed to clean up the lake. No one knew if the ecosystem could be saved. After they found that the lake's worst enemy was the phosphate in laundry soap, people protested until the soap makers removed the chemical. New laws required waste to go through a treatment plant before entering the lake. The two nations spent $8 billion to help clean Lake Erie.

After ten years the quality of Lake Erie's water had improved so much that it could be restocked with fish. People could once again swim in the lake. Even so, still more must be done to protect the lake and keep its water clean.

Recently scientists were alarmed to discover a "dead zone" in the lake. In this dead zone, the lake has low levels of oxygen and no living things—except for algae. Even outside the dead zone, more than 300 chemicals still pollute the lake to some degree. This causes problems for wildlife. For example, ospreys have such thin eggshells that few of their young hatch. Male whitefish do not develop normally. Scientists are doing research to determine what to do to solve these problems.

Lake Erie's Struggle to Survive *(cont.)*

Comprehension Questions

1. Lake Erie belongs to

ⓐ a Native American tribe.　　ⓒ the U.S.A.

ⓑ Canada.　　ⓓ both Canada and the U.S.A.

2. On a historical timeline, what happened third?

ⓐ Lake Erie "died."

ⓑ Soap makers removed phosphates from their products.

ⓒ People refused to buy laundry soap containing phosphates.

ⓓ Water quality in Lake Erie improved.

3. The Cuyahoga River in Ohio actually caught fire in 1969. How is this river similar to Lake Erie?

ⓐ both are huge bodies of water in the U.S.A.

ⓑ both bodies of water burned

ⓒ both bodies of water were severely polluted

ⓓ both bodies of water were never cleaned up

4. *Diluted* means

ⓐ treated.　　ⓒ cleansed.

ⓑ reduced.　　ⓓ increased.

5. From this article you can tell that

ⓐ a lake's ecosystem will try to rebalance itself once people stop abusing it.

ⓑ a lake that has died can never be brought back to life.

ⓒ all of the Great Lakes will eventually end up in the same condition as Lake Erie.

ⓓ most of Lake Erie's wildlife became extinct.

6. Picture Lake Erie's dead zone. What isn't in its water?

ⓐ clumps of algae　　ⓒ muskrats

ⓑ dead fish　　ⓓ rotting plants

7. Would you eat fish that have been caught in Lake Erie today? Explain.

_____

_____

_____

History Standard: Understands the United States territorial expansion between 1801 and 1861, and how it affected relations with external powers and Native Americans

Benchmark: Understands the factors that led to U.S. territorial expansion in the Western Hemisphere

The California Gold Rush

Gold is a rare metal. People have valued it for thousands of years. Even before gold was used as money, kings and queens wore it as jewelry. Many people dreamed of discovering a gold mine. Whenever gold has been found, it caused a gold rush. During a gold rush lots of people hurry to a place where gold was discovered. All over the world, wherever gold was found, the population grew quickly.

The biggest gold rush in American history happened when a man found gold in California in 1848. People raced across a vast wilderness to get to the West Coast. Some came from other countries, hoping to strike it rich. Once a person arrived, he had to stake a claim on a piece of land. Then any gold there belonged to him. Some people panned for gold by using a sieve. Sometimes the gold had to be dug out of the ground.

Since so many gold miners came to California during 1849, people called them the "forty-niners." Almost overnight San Francisco changed from a tiny town into a city of 25,000 people! So many people came to the area that California had enough people to become a state by 1850.

This wasn't the only gold rush. During the rest of the 1800s, large numbers of people went to other parts of the western United States and Alaska in search of gold. In places that had very little gold, the mines were emptied within a year or two. Then the people left the villages that had sprung up around these mines. After everyone moved away, people called these empty towns "ghost towns."

America changed due to the swift movement of many people to the West. People made roads, built homes, and created new towns in a matter of months. This caused fights between the **newcomers** and the Native Americans. The Native Americans did not want the settlers to come west. They wanted to go on with their way of life, following buffalo herds for food. The new roads went right through the areas where Native Americans lived and hunted. The gold miners did not want other people on their land. The Native Americans couldn't understand this. They did not believe that a person could own land. Unfortunately, the two groups usually did not work things out peacefully.

The California Gold Rush *(cont.)*

Comprehension Questions

1. In 1849 the majority of people journeying to California went to

  ⓐ get the area admitted to the Union as a state.

  ⓑ look for oil.

  ⓒ find gold.

  ⓓ get free farmland.

2. On a historical timeline, what happened second?

  ⓐ Most gold mines petered out.

  ⓑ Thousands of men raced to California.

  ⓒ Someone found gold in California.

  ⓓ California had enough people to qualify for statehood.

3. Why do people seek gold?

  ⓐ because they want to be royalty

  ⓑ because they want to be famous

  ⓒ because they want to be healthy

  ⓓ because they want to be wealthy

4. *Newcomers* are people

  ⓐ who are young.   ⓒ who have just arrived.

  ⓑ who just got married.   ⓓ who are ambitious.

5. What was certain to open up in a newly formed gold mining town?

  ⓐ a general store   ⓒ a train station

  ⓑ a doctor's office   ⓓ a newspaper office

6. Picture a '49 miner looking for gold. What tool is he using?

  ⓐ a jackhammer   ⓒ a rake

  ⓑ a backhoe   ⓓ a pickax

7. If you had been alive in the 1840s, would you have raced to California to search for gold? Explain.

_____

_____

_____

History Standard: Understands the causes and course of World War II, the character of the war at home and abroad, and its reshaping of the U.S. role in world affairs

Benchmark: Understands significant military aspects of World War II (e.g. major turning point of the war, locations of major theaters of war in the Pacific)

The Battle of Midway

The U.S. entered World War II after the Japanese made a surprise attack at a major naval base in Pearl Harbor in Hawaii. Their attack destroyed so many American ships and planes that the American navy was nearly wiped out.

The Japanese planned to get rid of the remaining ships with an **ambush**. They planned to attack Midway Island in the Pacific Ocean. They knew that the U.S. would have to defend the island. If it fell to the Japanese, they would have a good base for strikes against Hawaii and the West Coast.

The Japanese had four aircraft carriers. The Americans had three. Since planes could take off and land on them, these ships were the biggest and most important ones. Most of the battle was fought in the air by planes. When the planes needed fuel or ammunition, they returned to their ships.

The Japanese shot down almost 100 American planes. It looked certain that they would win. Suddenly, more American bombers came out of the cloud cover. They attacked the Japanese aircraft carriers. Immediately, three of the Japanese ships were almost completely destroyed and the fourth one badly damaged. The Americans lost an aircraft carrier, too. Many planes had to crash land in the ocean because they had no ship to land on.

Before this battle, America had been losing the war in the Pacific. Midway was the first Japanese defeat. It turned the tide of the war in the Pacific in America's favor.

The Battle of Midway (cont.)

Comprehension Questions

1. **Aircraft carriers were important because**

    ⓐ they moved faster than any other kind of ship.

    ⓑ they could transport jets far from land bases.

    ⓒ they couldn't sink.

    ⓓ they carried large numbers of soldiers into battle.

2. **On a historical timeline, what happened second?**

    ⓐ Four of the Japanese aircraft carriers were damaged or destroyed.

    ⓑ The Japanese attacked Pearl Harbor.

    ⓒ The Japanese shot down nearly 100 American planes over the Pacific Ocean.

    ⓓ The Japanese attacked Midway Island.

3. **Why did the U.S.A. defend Midway?**

    ⓐ The U.S.A. owned Midway Island.

    ⓑ America had promised the Midway islanders that they would be protected from the Japanese.

    ⓒ America couldn't afford to let their enemy have a place from which they could easily attack the mainland.

    ⓓ The American government had a lot of gold stored on the island.

4. **An *ambush* is**

    ⓐ a surprise attack.   ⓑ a battle that is fought only on the ground.

    ⓒ a war for a just cause.   ⓓ a fight in which one side has a lot more weapons.

5. **How do you think most Americans felt when they first heard the outcome of the Battle of Midway?**

    ⓐ worried   ⓑ relieved   ⓒ scared   ⓓ honored

6. **Picture an aircraft carrier. Why is its deck longer than a football field?**

    ⓐ because a large ship is less apt to be attacked by an enemy

    ⓑ because the bigger the ship, the faster it can move

    ⓒ because it has a huge variety of weapons on board

    ⓓ because it has a runway for jets to take off and land

7. **Do you think it's okay to fight and kill others in order to protect your country? Explain.**

    _____

    _____

    _____

History Standard: Understands how post-World War II reconstruction occurred, new international power relations took shape, and colonial empires broke up

Benchmark: Understands the development of the Cold War

The Berlin Wall

World War II ended when the Allied nations defeated the Axis nations of Germany, Italy, and Japan. When a war ends, the winners occupy the loser's country in order to establish control. Once things are running smoothly, they leave. After the war the Communist Soviets occupied East Berlin, Germany. Other Allied nations occupied other parts of the city. But when the rest of the Allied nations left, the Communists did not. Instead they renamed the area East Germany. Then in August 1961 they cut the phone lines, ended mail service, and shut down the border. No one could go into East Germany. No one could come out. If a child was visiting her grandparents in East Germany, she could not go home to her parents in West Germany. If a man was on business in West Germany, he could not get back to his family in East Germany. It took some families years to be reunited.

Work began on the Berlin Wall. The 20-foot (6 m) high cement wall had barbed wire on top. The Wall had 250 watch towers and 14,000 soldiers and dogs guarding it. Over the next 20 years, almost 600 East Germans died trying to cross it. Called the "Iron Curtain," its purpose was to keep the people under Communist control. It split Europe in two. On the west side was freedom. On the east side was Communism. This caused the Cold War of fear and **suspicion** between the Americans and the Soviets.

By the late 1980s the Soviets knew that they must find a way to feed their starving citizens. The government turned all of its attention to the matter. So when Hungary tore down its barbed wire barrier with Austria in March 1989, the Soviets did nothing. More than 150,000 East Germans left by this route. Another 1.8 million applied to leave. Then the Soviet government said they would reopen the border. As of midnight November 9, 1989, East Germans could cross the border for the first time in 28 years. Before midnight, an excited crowd took sledgehammers to the Wall. At midnight they slammed their hammers into the Wall. They danced and sang for two whole days. Today little remains of the Wall. Germany is reunited, and people move freely throughout the country.

The Berlin Wall *(cont.)*

Comprehension Questions

1. The Berlin Wall was destroyed in

(a) 1961.   (c) 1989.

(b) 1980.   (d) 2000.

2. On a historical timeline, what happened third?

(a) The Berlin Wall was built.

(b) Phone and mail service to East Germany ceased.

(c) The Allies occupied Germany.

(d) The Soviets would not leave East Germany.

3. Why didn't the Soviets react when Hungary and Austria destroyed their barrier?

(a) The Soviet government didn't know that it had happened.

(b) The Soviet government didn't have any way to stop them.

(c) All of the Soviet soldiers had fled the country.

(d) The Soviet government had other, more pressing problems.

4. A synonym for *suspicion* is

(a) distrust.   (c) loyalty.

(b) secrecy.   (d) disgust.

5. You can infer that the Soviets built the Berlin Wall because

(a) they wanted to make the world's biggest monument.

(b) they didn't want people to be able to leave the country.

(c) they wanted to stop illegal immigrants from entering Communist territory.

(d) they were ordered to do so by Adolf Hitler.

6. Picture the people destroying the Berlin Wall. What is the expression on their faces?

(a) confusion   (c) joy

(b) worry   (d) sorrow

7. Do you think that the Berlin Wall made Communism look stronger or weaker to the rest of the world? Explain.

_____

_____

_____

History Standard: Understands how the rise of corporations, heavy industry, and mechanized farming transformed American society

Benchmark: Understands the impact of significant achievements and individuals of the late 19th century

Let There Be Light!

For hundreds of years people used gas or oil lamps for light. These lamps were not very bright, and their open flames often caused house fires. So two men—one on each side of the Atlantic Ocean—tried to make an electric light bulb. Joseph Swan was English. Thomas Edison was American.

Inside a light bulb, electricity flows through a thin strip of material called a filament. As the filament glows white-hot, it gives off light. Edison and Swan tested many different things—from paper to iron—for filaments. Each material they used either did not light or caught on fire. Then, at almost the same time, Swan and Edison tried a carbon filament. Edison used burnt sewing thread. His carbon filament worked so well that the bulb stayed lit for several hours. Within four years, Edison made a bulb that glowed for 1,200 hours. Today, most light bulbs last around 2,000 hours.

Thomas Edison

Swan got a **patent** for his light bulb in 1878. Edison got his patent the next year. At first the two men accused each other of stealing ideas. Later on they decided to work together. They started a power company that still provides electricity to the New York City area.

Thomas Edison wanted electric lights to be common. This meant that he needed to bring electricity into people's homes. So he built the world's first electric power plant near Wall Street in New York City. In 1882 the Pearl Street Power Station used steam to make electric power for 203 homes. Electric lights quickly became so popular that within just a few years, thousands of homes had electricity. Today, almost every American home has electric lights.

Let There Be Light! *(cont.)*

Comprehension Questions

1. **What did Edison use for his first successful filament?**

   (a) burnt sewing thread   (c) waxed string

   (b) copper wire   (d) plastic twine

2. **On a historical timeline, what happened second?**

   (a) Edison got a patent for an electric light bulb.

   (b) Swan got a patent for an electric light bulb.

   (c) Swan and Edison worked together.

   (d) Swan and Edison accused each other of stealing ideas.

3. **Compared to Edison's 1882 light bulb, modern light bulbs last**

   (a) slightly less time.   (c) about the same length of time.

   (b) several thousand hours longer.   (d) almost 1,000 hours longer.

4. **An example of something that a person would get a *patent* for is**

   (a) writing a new song.   (c) creating a device to store photos.

   (b) compiling a dictionary.   (d) producing a movie.

5. **Electric lights were safer than previous lighting because light bulbs**

   (a) gave light in any kind of weather.

   (b) gave light without a flame.

   (c) did not use animal fat.

   (d) could not burn out.

6. **Picture an empty light socket. What must you be careful not to do?**

   (a) screw a light bulb into the socket

   (b) put a black light bulb into the socket

   (c) let dust get into the empty socket

   (d) stick your finger into the socket

7. **Do you think that Joseph Swan should receive credit for inventing the electric light bulb? Explain.**

   _____

   _____

   _____

History Standard: Understands the economic boom and social transformation of post-World War II United States

Benchmark: Understands the impact of postwar scientific research on contemporary society

Satellites

After World War II ended, people found new ways to use the things developed for the war. Radar had been invented to track enemy planes. Police started using radar to watch for speeding cars. The people who report our weather used radar to track storms. For years, radar was the only thing that watched the skies.

Then President Kennedy decided that an American should land on the moon. He provided funds to NASA (National Aeronautics and Space Administration) to run the space program. In addition to space flights, NASA has put many satellites into orbit. Satellites stay at a specific height and move at a specific speed as they circle our planet. The Earth's gravity holds them in orbit. We rely on these satellites every day.

Six kinds of satellites orbit our planet. Earth observation satellites keep track of the conditions of oceans, icebergs, volcanoes, and deserts. They also track forest fires and animal herds. Spy satellites watch military movements. Weather satellites record cloud movements and wind speeds. Global Positioning System (GPS) satellites let cars, planes, and ships know their **precise** position on the Earth. Astronomy satellites keep track of the sun, stars, and comets.

Communications satellites get signals from computers, telephones, and TV cameras. Then they send these signals to another computer, phone, or TV. They handle e-mails and long-distance phone calls. They let you watch what's happening in another part of the world while it's happening.

Out in space the sun always shines because there is no night or clouds. So satellites use solar cell power. The solar cells collect the sun's rays and change them into electricity. Solar cells work for many years, and astronauts on the space shuttle can go up and fix them if there is a problem.

Satellites *(cont.)*

Comprehension Questions

1. **Which is not a kind of satellite?**

   (a) solar   (c) communications

   (b) weather   (d) spy

2. **On a historical timeline, what happened third?**

   (a) President Kennedy provided funds to NASA.

   (b) Satellites were put into orbit.

   (c) Radar was used to forecast the weather.

   (d) Astronauts learned how to repair satellites.

3. **Which is an example of a naturally occurring satellite?**

   (a) Halley's comet   (c) one of Jupiter's moons

   (b) the sun   (d) an asteroid

4. ***Precise* means**

   (a) approximate.   (c) exact.

   (b) general.   (d) closest.

5. **A satellite's solar cells receive energy**

   (a) from alkaline batteries.

   (b) only during daylight hours.

   (c) a different number of hours each season.

   (d) 24 hours every day.

6. **Picture a satellite. What is it made of?**

   (a) canvas   (c) marble

   (b) aluminum   (d) wood

7. **Would you like to be one of the astronauts who fixes satellites out in space? Explain.**

   _____

   _____

   _____

History Standard: Understands the United States territorial expansion between 1801 and 1861, and how it affected relations with external powers and Native Americans

Benchmark: Knows the foreign territorial claims in the Western Hemisphere in the 1800s and the impact on American foreign policy

Mexico: Past and Present

Hundreds of years ago, Native-American tribes lived in Mexico. The Aztecs built beautiful cities. They had a calendar and a written language. However, the Spanish destroyed the Aztecs in 1521. For the next 300 years, Spain ruled over Mexico. That's why Mexicans speak Spanish.

Every September 16 the Mexican people hold a celebration in Mexico City, their country's capital. It is their Independence Day. On that date in 1821 they told Spain they would no longer be ruled. Breaking free from Spain caused a war. When it was over, the Mexicans had their own government. They made their own laws.

Today America and Mexico are friends, but it wasn't always that way. President James Polk wanted America to reach from the Atlantic Ocean to the Pacific Ocean. He tried to buy what is now the American southwest from Mexico. Mexico would not sell. So from 1846 to 1848 Mexico and America fought a war to **ascertain** where their borders would be. When the war ended, Mexico had lost a lot of land. Now the Rio Grande River forms the border between the two nations. America is on the north side of the river. Mexico is on the south side.

Mexico has mountains and a hot, dry climate. Crops can grow on only a small part of the land. Still, Mexicans grow much of the coffee, oranges, and sugar used in the U.S. Mexicans have influenced building styles in southwestern U.S. and added words such as patio and canyon to our language. Americans also enjoy eating many Mexican foods like burritos, tacos, tortillas, and tamales.

Mexico: Past and Present (cont.)

Comprehension Questions

1. **President Polk wanted**

   (a) the U.S. to expand its borders.

   (b) Mexico to change its Independence Day to July 4th.

   (c) the country of Mexico to become one of the states of the Union.

   (d) Americans to adopt the Mexican language.

2. **On a historical timeline, what happened second?**

   (a) Mexicans declared their independence from Spain.

   (b) The Spanish lived in Mexico.

   (c) The Aztecs lived in Mexico.

   (d) Americans fought a war with Mexico.

3. **How long after America declared its independence from England did Mexico do the same with Spain?**

   (a) about the same time   (c) about a century

   (b) about 50 years   (d) about 150 years

4. **Another word for *ascertain* is**

   (a) inspect.   (c) discover.

   (b) change.   (d) determine.

5. **Before the Aztecs were conquered, these Native Americans probably**

   (a) didn't speak Spanish.

   (b) couldn't read or write any language.

   (c) had no tools.

   (d) didn't understand the concept of time.

6. **Picture the ancient Aztec cities. What are the buildings made of?**

   (a) wood   (c) stone blocks

   (b) straw   (d) steel

7. **Do you think the American government was right to declare war on Mexico after that nation refused to sell its land in 1846? Explain.**

   _____

   _____

   _____

Answer Key

Page 9	Page 17	Page 25	Page 33	Page 41
1. a	1. c	1. d	1. a	1. c
2. c	2. a	2. b	2. c	2. b
3. c	3. b	3. a	3. d	3. d
4. d	4. c	4. c	4. b	4. a
5. a	5. a	5. d	5. b	5. b
6. b	6. d	6. a	6. d	6. c
7. Accept well-supported answers.	7. Accept well-supported answers.	7. Accept well-supported answers.	7. Accept well-supported answers.	7. Accept well-supported answers.

Page 11	Page 19	Page 27	Page 35	Page 43
1. c	1. a	1. b	1. d	1. a
2. b	2. c	2. a	2. b	2. a
3. a	3. c	3. c	3. c	3. d
4. d	4. b	4. a	4. b	4. c
5. c	5. a	5. d	5. a	5. b
6. c	6. d	6. b	6. c	6. d
7. Accept well-supported answers.	7. Accept well-supported answers.	7. Accept well-supported answers.	7. Accept well-supported answers.	7. Accept well-supported answers.

Page 13	Page 21	Page 29	Page 37	Page 45
1. b	1. b	1. b	1. c	1. a
2. c	2. c	2. a	2. b	2. b
3. b	3. a	3. c	3. d	3. c
4. d	4. d	4. b	4. c	4. c
5. c	5. c	5. c	5. a	5. d
6. a	6. a	6. d	6. d	6. b
7. Accept well-supported answers.	7. Accept well-supported answers.	7. Accept well-supported answers.	7. Accept well-supported answers.	7. Accept well-supported answers.

Page 15	Page 23	Page 31	Page 39	Page 47
1. d	1. d	1. c	1. b	1. a
2. c	2. a	2. c	2. d	2. b
3. b	3. b	3. d	3. c	3. b
4. a	4. c	4. a	4. a	4. d
5. b	5. a	5. b	5. b	5. a
6. c	6. d	6. d	6. d	6. c
7. Accept well-supported answers.	7. Accept well-supported answers.	7. Accept well-supported answers.	7. Accept well-supported answers.	7. Accept well-supported answers.